Verses of a V.

Vera Brittain

Alpha Editions

This edition published in 2024

ISBN : 9789362925794

Design and Setting By
Alpha Editions
www.alphaedis.com
Email - info@alphaedis.com

As per information held with us this book is in Public Domain.
This book is a reproduction of an important historical work. Alpha Editions uses the best technology to reproduce historical work in the same manner it was first published to preserve its original nature. Any marks or number seen are left intentionally to preserve its true form.

Contents

FOREWORD ....- 1 -
AUGUST 1914 ....- 3 -
ST. PANCRAS STATION, AUGUST 1915 ....- 3 -
TO A FALLEN IDOL ....- 3 -
TO MONSEIGNEUR ....- 4 -
THE ONLY SON..- 4 -
PERHAPS—— ....- 5 -
A MILITARY HOSPITAL..- 6 -
LOOKING WESTWARD ....- 6 -
THEN AND NOW...- 7 -
MAY MORNING ....- 7 -
THE TWO TRAVELLERS ....- 8 -
ROUNDEL ....- 9 -
THE SISTERS BURIED AT LEMNOS........................- 9 -
IN MEMORIAM: G.R.Y.T. ....- 10 -
A PARTING WORD ....- 11 -
TO MY BROTHER[A]..- 11 -
SIC TRANSIT—— ....- 12 -
TO THEM ....- 13 -
OXFORD REVISITED ....- 13 -
THAT WHICH REMAINETH.....................................- 14 -
THE GERMAN WARD ....- 14 -
THE TROOP-TRAIN ....- 15 -
TO MY WARD-SISTER ....- 16 -
TO ANOTHER SISTER...- 16 -
"VENGEANCE IS MINE"..- 17 -

WAR	- 17 -
THE LAST POST	- 18 -
THE ASPIRANT	- 18 -

FOREWORD

THESE poems, by a writer for whom I have literary hopes, belong very clearly to that new and vigorous type of poetry which has sprung from the stress of the last few years and has its root in things done and suffered rather than in things merely imagined.

Until lately our very belief in the saying that the poet is born and not made proved that we had completely accepted poetry as coming only from within, spun, as it were, out of our inner consciousness, and either quite unhelped, or else only partially helped, by active experiences from without. We have always understood, of course, that such an experience as, for instance, the sudden flashing upon us of a magnetic face as a stranger passes in the street might set aglow a train of thought that would quicken and melt into feeling, and the feeling would, in turn, need—and find—expression in poetry.

So far as this we have admitted that outward occurrences in the course of our quickly flying days can become a source of poetical inspiration. But, in spite of the pointing finger of Kipling, most of us clung desperately to the verse that had its sole origin in imaginative emotion until the blaze of war in the world illumined our souls and showed all of us that out of our simplest practical work can be struck sparks of real and great and rare divine fire.

All the poems in this little book are the outcome of things very deeply felt. It is very difficult for me to write of them because where there is pain uttered in them, it has almost always been my pain as well as the author's. One or two of the sonnets condense the expression of losses that have meant a life's upheaval. One or two, again, are practically a concrete record of simple human things observed and suffered and of duty strenuously done. Here there is no leisured dreaming, but sheer experience, solid and stored up, like the honey that a bee's labour has stored.

But this practical quality, while it has so much that makes it rich and valuable, has also the one conspicuous disadvantage that the work is often done under conditions of strain and turmoil that tell against perfection of method. Some of these *Verses of a V.A.D.* were written in almost breathless intervals of severe and devoted duty. The poem entitled "The German Ward" is especially an example of this. In such circumstances, it is difficult to achieve any literary ornamentation and least of all that particular kind of simpleness which is the highest form of finished art. In the case of several of the poems, both these qualities have been achieved; yet, because of the difficulties, I make an appeal for considerateness and tender sympathy in judging these first shy flowers of the heart and mind of a young girl who has worked unceasingly and self-forgettingly for the good of others since the days of stress began, and who in her personal destiny has suffered as, I hope, very few have suffered.

MARIE CONNOR LEIGHTON.

AUGUST 1914

GOD said, "Men have forgotten Me;
The souls that sleep shall wake again,
And blinded eyes must learn to see."

So since redemption comes through pain
He smote the earth with chastening rod,
And brought Destruction's lurid reign;

But where His desolation trod
The people in their agony
Despairing cried, "There is no God."

SOMERVILLE COLLEGE,
OXFORD.

ST. PANCRAS STATION, AUGUST 1915

ONE long, sweet kiss pressed close upon my lips,
One moment's rest on your swift-beating heart,
And all was over, for the hour had come
For us to part.

A sudden forward motion of the train,
The world grown dark although the sun still shone,
One last blurred look through aching tear-dimmed eyes—
And you were gone.

TO A FALLEN IDOL

O YOU who sought to rend the stars from Heaven
But rent instead your too-ambitious heart,
Know that with those to whom Love's joy is given
You have not, nor can ever have, a part.

A nation's loyalty might have been your glory,
And men have blessed your name from shore to shore,
But you have set the seal upon your story,

And must go hence, alone for evermore.

TO MONSEIGNEUR

(R.A.L., LIEUTENANT, WORCESTERS)

NONE shall dispute Your kingship, nor declare
Another could have held the place You hold,
For though he brought me finer gifts than gold,
And laid before my feet his heart made bare
Of all but love for me, and sighed despair
If I but feigned my favours to withhold,
And would repudiate as sadly cold
The proud and lofty manner that You wear,

He would not be my pure and stainless knight
Of heart without reproach or hint of fear,
Who walks unscathed amid War's sordid ways
By base desire or bloodshed's grim delight,
But ever holds his hero's honour dear—
Roland of Roncesvalles in modern days.

1ST LONDON GENERAL HOSPITAL,
November 1915.

THE ONLY SON

THE storm beats loud, and you are far away,
The night is wild,
On distant fields of battle breaks the day,
My little child?

I sought to shield you from the least of ills
In bygone years,
I soothed with dreams of manhood's far-off hills
Your baby fears,

But could not save you from the shock of strife;
With radiant eyes

You seized the sword and in the path of Life
You sought your prize.

The tempests rage, but you are fast asleep;
Though winds be wild
They cannot break your endless slumbers deep,
My little child.

PERHAPS——

(TO R.A.L. DIED OF WOUNDS IN FRANCE, DECEMBER 23RD, 1915)

PERHAPS some day the sun will shine again,
And I shall see that still the skies are blue,
And feel once more I do not live in vain,
Although bereft of You.

Perhaps the golden meadows at my feet
Will make the sunny hours of Spring seem gay,
And I shall find the white May blossoms sweet,
Though You have passed away.

Perhaps the summer woods will shimmer bright,
And crimson roses once again be fair,
And autumn harvest fields a rich delight,
Although You are not there.

Perhaps some day I shall not shrink in pain
To see the passing of the dying year,
And listen to the Christmas songs again,
Although You cannot hear.

But, though kind Time may many joys renew,
There is one greatest joy I shall not know
Again, because my heart for loss of You
Was broken, long ago.

1ST LONDON GENERAL HOSPITAL,
February 1916.

A MILITARY HOSPITAL

A MASS of human wreckage, drifting in
Borne on a blood-red tide,
Some never more to brave the stormy sea
Laid reverently aside,
And some with love restored to sail again
For regions far and wide.

1ST LONDON GENERAL HOSPITAL, *1916*.

LOOKING WESTWARD

"For a while the quiet body
Lies with feet toward the Morn."
HYMN 499, A. & M.

WHEN I am dead, lay me not looking East,
But towards the verge where daylight sinks to rest,
For my Beloved, who fell in War's dark year,
Lies in a foreign meadow, facing West.

He does not see the Heavens flushed with dawn,
But flaming through the sunset's dying gleam;
He is not dazzled by the Morning Star,
But Hesper soothes him with her gentle beam.

He faces not the guns he thrilled to hear,
Nor sees the skyline red with fires of Hell;
He looks for ever towards that dear home land
He loved, but bade a resolute farewell.

So would I, when my hour has come for sleep,
Lie watching where the twilight shades grow grey;
Far sooner would I share with him the Night
Than pass without him to the Splendid Day.

THEN AND NOW

"πάντα ῥει καὶ οὐδένα μένει"

ONCE the black pine-trees on the mountain side,
The river dancing down the valley blue,
And strange brown grasses swaying with the tide,
All spoke to me of you.

But now the sullen streamlet creeping slow,
The moaning tree-tops dark above my head,
The weeds where once the grasses used to grow
Tell me that you are dead.

MAY MORNING

(*Note.*—At Oxford on May 1st a Latin hymn is sung at sunrise by the Magdalen choristers from the top of the tower.)

THE rising sun shone warmly on the tower,
Into the clear pure Heaven the hymn aspired
Piercingly sweet. This was the morning hour
When life awoke with Spring's creative power,
And the old City's grey to gold was fired.

Silently reverent stood the noisy throng;
Under the bridge the boats in long array
Lay motionless. The choristers' far song
Faded upon the breeze in echoes long.
Swiftly I left the bridge and rode away.

Straight to a little wood's green heart I sped,
Where cowslips grew, beneath whose gold withdrawn
The fragrant earth peeped warm and richly red;
All trace of Winter's chilling touch had fled,
And song-birds ushered in the year's bright morn.

I had met Love not many days before,
And as in blissful mood I listening lay
None ever had of joy so full a store.
I thought that Spring must last for evermore,

For I was young and loved, and it was May.
. . . .
Now it is May again, and sweetly clear
Perhaps once more aspires the Latin hymn
From Magdalen tower, but not for me to hear.
I toil far distant, for a darker year
Shadows the century with menace grim.

I walk in ways where pain and sorrow dwell,
And ruin such as only War can bring,
Where each lives through his individual hell,
Fraught with remembered horror none can tell,
And no more is there glory in the Spring.

And I am worn with tears, for he I loved
Lies cold beneath the stricken sod of France;
Hope has forsaken me, by Death removed,
And Love that seemed so strong and gay has proved
A poor crushed thing, the toy of cruel Chance.

Often I wonder, as I grieve in vain,
If when the long, long future years creep slow,
And War and tears alike have ceased to reign,
I ever shall recapture, once again,
The mood of that May morning, long ago.

1ST LONDON GENERAL HOSPITAL,
May 1916.

THE TWO TRAVELLERS

Beware!
You met two travellers in the town
Who promised you that they would take you down
The valley far away
To some strange carnival this Summer's day.
Take care,
Lest in the crowded street
They hurry past you with forgetting feet,
And leave you standing there.

ROUNDEL

("Died of Wounds")

Because you died, I shall not rest again,
But wander ever through the lone world wide,
Seeking the shadow of a dream grown vain
Because you died.

I shall spend brief and idle hours beside
The many lesser loves that still remain,
But find in none my triumph and my pride;

And Disillusion's slow corroding stain
Will creep upon each quest but newly tried,
For every striving now shall nothing gain
Because you died.

France,
February 1918.

THE SISTERS BURIED AT LEMNOS

("Fidelis ad Extremum")

O golden Isle set in the deep blue Ocean,
With purple shadows flitting o'er thy crest,
I kneel to thee in reverent devotion
Of some who on thy bosom lie at rest!

Seldom they enter into song or story;
Poets praise the soldier's might and deeds of War,
But few exalt the Sisters, and the glory
Of women dead beneath a distant star.

No armies threatened in that lonely station,
They fought not fire or steel or ruthless foe,
But heat and hunger, sickness and privation,
And Winter's deathly chill and blinding snow.

Till mortal frailty could endure no longer
Disease's ravages and climate's power,
In body weak, but spirit ever stronger,
Courageously they stayed to meet their hour.

No blazing tribute through the wide world flying,
No rich reward of sacrifice they craved,
The only meed of their victorious dying
Lives in the hearts of humble men they saved.

Who when in light the Final Dawn is breaking,
Still faithful, though the world's regard may cease,
Will honour, splendid in triumphant waking,
The souls of women, lonely here at peace.

O golden Isle with purple shadows falling
Across thy rocky shore and sapphire sea,
I shall not picture these without recalling
The Sisters sleeping on the heart of thee!

H.M.H.S. "BRITANNIC," MUDROS,
October 1916.

IN MEMORIAM: G.R.Y.T.

(KILLED IN ACTION, APRIL 23RD, 1917)

I SPOKE with you but seldom, yet there lay
Some nameless glamour in your written word,
And thoughts of you rose often—longings stirred
By dear remembrance of the sad blue-grey
That dwelt within your eyes, the even sway
Of your young god-like gait, the rarely heard
But frank bright laughter, hallowed by a Day
That made of Youth Right's offering to the sword.

So now I ponder, since your day is done,
Ere dawn was past, on all you meant to me,
And all the more you might have come to be,
And wonder if some state, beyond the sun

And shadows here, may yet completion see
Of intimacy sweet though scarce begun.

MALTA,
May 1917.

A PARTING WORD

(TO A FORTUNATE FRIEND)

IF you should be too happy in your days
And never know an hour of vain regret,
Do not forget
That still the shadows darken all my ways.

If sunshine sweeter still should light your years,
And you lose nought of all you dearly prize,
Turn not your eyes
From my steep track of anguish and of tears.

And if perhaps your love of me is less
Than I with all my need of you would choose,
Do not refuse
To love enough to lighten my distress.

And if the future days should parting see
Of our so different paths that lately met,
Remember yet
Those days of storm you weathered through with me.

MALTA,
May 1917.

TO MY BROTHER[A]

(IN MEMORY OF JULY 1ST, 1916)

YOUR battle-wounds are scars upon my heart,
Received when in that grand and tragic "show"

You played your part
Two years ago,

And silver in the summer morning sun
I see the symbol of your courage glow—
That Cross you won
Two years ago.

Though now again you watch the shrapnel fly,
And hear the guns that daily louder grow,
As in July
Two years ago,

May you endure to lead the Last Advance
And with your men pursue the flying foe
As once in France
Two years ago.

[A] Captain E. H. Brittain, M.C. Written four days before his death in action in the Austrian offensive on the Italian Front, June 15th, 1918.

SIC TRANSIT——

(V.R., DIED OF WOUNDS, 2ND LONDON GENERAL HOSPITAL, CHELSEA,
JUNE 9TH, 1917)

I AM so tired.
The dying sun incarnadines the West,
And every window with its gold is fired,
And all I loved the best
Is gone, and every good that I desired
Passes away, an idle hopeless quest;
Even the Highest whereto I aspired
Has vanished with the rest.
I am so tired.

LONDON,
June 1917.

TO THEM

I HEAR your voices in the whispering trees,
I see your footprints on each grassy track,
Your laughter echoes gaily down the breeze—
But you will not come back.

The twilight skies are tender with your smile,
The stars look down with eyes for which I yearn,
I dream that you are with me all the while—
But you will not return.

The flowers are gay in gardens that you knew,
The woods you loved are sweet with summer rain,
The fields you trod are empty now, but you
Will never come again.

June 1917.

OXFORD REVISITED

THERE'S a gleam of sun on the grey old street
Where we used to walk in the Oxford days,
And dream that the world lay beneath our feet
In the dawn of a summer morning.

Now the years have passed, and it's we who lie
Crushed under the burden of world-wide woe,
But the misty magic will never die
From the dawn of an Oxford morning.

And the end delays, and perhaps no more
I shall see the spires of my youth's delight,
But they'll gladden my eyes as in days of yore
At the dawn of Eternal Morning.

June 1917.

THAT WHICH REMAINETH

(IN MEMORY OF CAPTAIN E. H. BRITTAIN, M.C.)

ONLY the thought of a merry smile,
The wistful dreaming of sad brown eyes—
A brave young warrior, face aglow
With the light of a lofty enterprise.

Only the hope of a gallant heart,
The steady strife for a deathless crown,
In Memory's treasures, radiant now
With the gleam of a goal beyond renown.

Only the tale of a dream fulfilled,
A strenuous day and a well-fought fight,
A fearless leader who laughed at Death,
And the fitting end of a gentle knight.

Only a Cross on a mountain side,
The close of a journey short and rough,
A sword laid down and a stainless shield—
No more—and yet, is it not enough?

THE GERMAN WARD

("INTER ARMA CARITAS")

WHEN the years of strife are over and my recollection fades
Of the wards wherein I worked the weeks away,
I shall still see, as a vision rising 'mid the War-time shades,
The ward in France where German wounded lay.

I shall see the pallid faces and the half-suspicious eyes,
I shall hear the bitter groans and laboured breath,
And recall the loud complaining and the weary tedious cries,
And sights and smells of blood and wounds and death.

I shall see the convoy cases, blanket-covered on the floor,
And watch the heavy stretcher-work begin,

And the gleam of knives and bottles through the open theatre door,
And the operation patients carried in.

I shall see the Sister standing, with her form of youthful grace,
And the humour and the wisdom of her smile,
And the tale of three years' warfare on her thin expressive face—
The weariness of many a toil-filled while.

I shall think of how I worked for her with nerve and heart and mind,
And marvelled at her courage and her skill,
And how the dying enemy her tenderness would find
Beneath her scornful energy of will.

And I learnt that human mercy turns alike to friend or foe
When the darkest hour of all is creeping nigh,
And those who slew our dearest, when their lamps were burning low,
Found help and pity ere they came to die.

So, though much will be forgotten when the sound of War's alarms
And the days of death and strife have passed away,
I shall always see the vision of Love working amidst arms
In the ward wherein the wounded prisoners lay.

FRANCE,
September 1917.

THE TROOP-TRAIN

(FRANCE, 1917)

As we came down from Amiens,
And they went up the line,
They waved their careless hands to us,
And cheered the Red Cross sign.

And often I have wondered since,
Repicturing that train,
How many of those laughing souls
Came down the line again.

TO MY WARD-SISTER

Night Duty, December 1917

THROUGH the night-watches of our House of Sighs
In capable serenity of mind
You steadily achieve the tasks designed
With calm, half-smiling, interested eyes;
Though all-unknowing, confidently wise
Concerning pain you never felt, you find
Content from uneventful years arise
As you toil on, mechanically kind.

So thus far have your smooth days passed, but when
The tempest none escape shall cloud your sky,
And Life grow dark around you, through your pain
You'll learn the meaning of your mercy then
To those who blessed you as you passed them by,
Nor seek to tread the untroubled road again.

France.

TO ANOTHER SISTER

I KNEW that you had suffered many things,
For I could see your eyes would often weep
Through bitter midnight hours when others sleep;
And in your smile the lurking scorn that springs
From cruel knowledge of a love, once deep,
Grown gradually cold, until the stings
Pierce mercilessly of a past that clings
Undying to your lonely path and steep.

So, loved and honoured leader, I would pray
That hidden future days may hold in store
Some solace for your yearning even yet,
And in some joy to come you may forget
The burdened toil you will not suffer more,
And see the War-time shadows fade away.

France, *1918*.

"VENGEANCE IS MINE"

(In Memory of the Sisters who died in the Great Air Raid upon Hospitals at Étaples)

Who shall avenge us for anguish unnamable,
Rivers of scarlet and crosses of grey,
Terror of night-time and blood-lust untamable,
Hate without pity where broken we lay?

How could we help them, in agony calling us,
Those whom we laboured to comfort and save,
How still their moaning, whose hour was befalling us,
Crushed in a horror more dark than the grave?

Burning of canvas and smashing of wood above—
Havoc of Mercy's toil—shall He forget
Us that have fallen, Who numbers in gracious love
Each tiny creature whose life is man's debt?

Will He not hear us, though speech is now failing us—
Voices too feeble to utter a cry?
Shall they not answer, the foemen assailing us,
Women who suffer and women who die?

Who shall avenge us for anguish unnamable,
Rivers of scarlet and crosses of grey,
Terror of night-time and blood-lust untamable,
Hate without pity where broken we lay?

WAR

(The Great German Offensive, March—May 1918)

A night of storm and thunder crashing by,
A bitter night of tempest and of rain—
Then calm at dawn beneath a wind-swept sky,
And broken flowers that will not bloom again.

An age of Death and Agony and Tears,
A cruel age of woe unguessed before—

Then peace to close the weary storm-wrecked years,
And broken hearts that bleed for evermore.

FRANCE.

THE LAST POST

THE stars are shining bright above the camps,
The bugle calls float skyward, faintly clear;
Over the hill the mist-veiled motor lamps
Dwindle and disappear.

The notes of day's good-bye arise and blend
With the low murmurous hum from tree and sod,
And swell into that question at the end
They ask each night of God—

Whether the dead within the burial ground
Will ever overthrow their crosses grey,
And rise triumphant from each lowly mound
To greet the dawning day.

Whether the eyes which battle sealed in sleep
Will open to reveillé once again,
And forms, once mangled, into rapture leap,
Forgetful of their pain.

But still the stars above the camp shine on,
Giving no answer for our sorrow's ease,
And one more day with the Last Post has gone
Dying upon the breeze.

ÉTAPLES, *1918.*

THE ASPIRANT

(A PLEA)

BECAUSE I dare to stand outside the gate
Of that high temple wherein Fame abides,

And loudly knock, too eager to await
Whate'er betides,

May God forgive, since He alone can see
The joys that others have but I must miss,
For how shall Compensation come to me
If not through this?

———————————

Milton Keynes UK
Ingram Content Group UK Ltd.
UKHW020825231024
450026UK00004B/393